Copyright © 2020 Kinnie Media Group
Published by Kinnie Media Group

No part of this publication may be reproduced, or stored in a retrieval system, or transmitted in any form or by any means, electronic, mechanical, recording, photocopying, scanning or otherwise, without express written permission of the publisher.

For permission to use this planner for a class or request a speaker, send email to: hello@motorcitywoman.com

Disclaimer

This book should only be used as a guide. The publisher makes no representations or warranties. For more in-depth advice, you should consult a professional. The publisher nor the author shall be liable for any loss of profit or any other commercial damages, including but not limited to special, incidental, consequential, or other damages.

Welcome

Welcome to the Motor City Woman Planner for New Podcasters! This guide is full of resources, tools and guides especially designed for the new podcaster. You can skip the hours of research looking for what you need to launch, maintain and grow your podcast. It's all here – in this handy planner.

HOW TO USE:

You will notice that this planner is missing a crucial part of most planners – a calendar! That's because this planner is for people who want to go at their own pace and set their own schedule. You may only record 2 episodes per month or 4 per week. Either way, you can use this guide to make sure you've done everything in your power to be successful.

This planner should be used to organize your thoughts, map out strategy and keep everything in one place. We have even included fill-in-the-blank templates ranging from communicating with guests to a monthly workflow. We've done all of the work so you, new podcaster, can concentrate on what's most important – amplifying your voice.

Thank you for bringing Motor City Woman with you along your journey. For more, visit motorcitywoman.com.

Happy Podcasting!

Robin Kinnie
Author

Why are you here?

First things first, you need to identify your WHY. Once you have defined your WHY, it will be easy to create content, identify guests and create a marketing strategy.

Why did you decide to launch a podcast?

_____
_____
_____
_____

Who do you want to reach with your podcast?

_____
_____
_____
_____

What do you want your listeners to feel?

_____
_____
_____
_____

What are your goals for the podcast?

_____
_____
_____
_____

Podcast Launch Checklist

- [ ] Podcast Name + Theme
- [ ] Cover Art
- [ ] Social Media Handles
- [ ] Website / Landing Page
- [ ] Recording Calendar
- [ ] Ideal Guests + Show Outlines
- [ ] Sponsorship Deck
- [ ] Trailer + 5 episodes recorded
- [ ] Podcast Safe music secured
- [ ] RSS feed set-up
- [ ]
- [ ]
- [ ]

Motor City Woman

For more resources, visit www.MotorCityWoman.com

PODCAST TERMINOLOGY

PODCAST
Think of "audio on-demand". The term originated from the Apple IPOD (pod-) and broadcast (-cast.)

STREAMING PLATFORM
This is the tool that distributes your podcast for consumption.

RSS FEED
Houses your audio files and, once connected to a streaming platform, publishes new episodes.

COVER ART
A graphic used to promote your podcast on streaming platforms.

POST-PRODUCTION
The process after a podcast episode is recorded. This may include adding music and removing mistakes.

TECH GEAR
You will need a combination of gear to produce a podcast - a microphone, recording device and editing software.

For more resources, visit www.MotorCityWoman.com

Brainstorm

Potential show topics

_____
_____
_____
_____
_____

Potential guests

_____
_____
_____
_____
_____

What I like about others podcasts

_____
_____
_____
_____
_____

What I don't like about other podcasts

_____
_____
_____
_____

Workflow for Each Month

01 Identify number of shows you're doing

02 Identify show topics

03 Research potential guests

04 Align with national holidays and current events

05 Match show topic with guest

06 Identify recording dates

07 Release new episodes

08 Research potential sponsors

09 Cultivate potential collaborations

10 Promote shows

For more resources, visit www.MotorCityWoman.com

> Speech has power. Words do not fade. What starts out as a sound; ends in a deed.
>
> - ABRAHAM JOSHUA HESCHEL

For more resources, visit www.MotorCityWoman.com

Month: ☐

What are your goals for this month?
_____
_____
_____
_____

How many show are you doing this month? ☐

Show: _____
Topic: _____
Guest: _____

Show: _____
Topic: _____
Guest: _____

Show: _____
Topic: _____
Guest: _____

Show: _____
Topic: _____
Guest: _____

Show: _____
Topic: _____
Guest: _____

For more resources, visit www.MotorCityWoman.com

Intentions Page

Success doesn't happen by accident. Use this space to set your intention or plan of action to achieve a successful podcast.

_____
_____
_____
_____
_____
_____
_____
_____
_____
_____
_____
_____
_____
_____
_____
_____
_____
_____
_____
_____

Punch List for each show

It can sometimes get difficult to do everything for each show. Luckily, you have this planner to keep you organized!

Before

- Identify show topic
- Confirm guest and recording date
- Send guest prep email
- Create outline

During

- Use outline to guide conversation
- Record show
- Mention advertisers, sponsors, etc.
- Promote your product or service
- Call-to-action for listeners

After

- Edit show
- Upload show to RSS feed (hosting site)
- Send thank you email to guest
- Promote show and repurpose content

Note: See back section of this journal for templates, outlines and guides.

 **Month:**

What are your goals for this month?
_____
_____
_____
_____

How many show are you doing this month? ☐

Show: _____
Topic: _____
Guest: _____

Show: _____
Topic: _____
Guest: _____

Show: _____
Topic: _____
Guest: _____

Show: _____
Topic: _____
Guest: _____

Show: _____
Topic: _____
Guest: _____

For more resources, visit www.MotorCityWoman.com

Intentions Page

Success doesn't happen by accident. Use this space to set your intention or plan of action to achieve a successful podcast.

_____
_____
_____
_____
_____
_____
_____
_____
_____
_____
_____
_____
_____
_____
_____
_____
_____
_____
_____
_____
_____

Punch List for each show

It can sometimes get difficult to do everything for each show. Luckily, you have this planner to keep you organized!

Before

- Identify show topic
- Confirm guest and recording date
- Send guest prep email
- Create outline

During

- Use outline to guide conversation
- Record show
- Mention advertisers, sponsors, etc.
- Promote your product or service
- Call-to-action for listeners

After

- Edit show
- Upload show to RSS feed (hosting site)
- Send thank you email to guest
- Promote show and repurpose content

Note: See back section of this journal for templates, outlines and guides.

For more resources, visit www.MotorCityWoman.com

Month: ☐

What are your goals for this month?
_____
_____
_____
_____

How many show are you doing this month? ☐

Show: _____
Topic: _____
Guest: _____

Show: _____
Topic: _____
Guest: _____

Show: _____
Topic: _____
Guest: _____

Show: _____
Topic: _____
Guest: _____

Show: _____
Topic: _____
Guest: _____

For more resources, visit www.MotorCityWoman.com

Intentions Page

Success doesn't happen by accident. Use this space to set your intention or plan of action to achieve a successful podcast.

Punch List for each show

It can sometimes get difficult to do everything for each show. Luckily, you have this planner to keep you organized!

Before

- Identify show topic
- Confirm guest and recording date
- Send guest prep email
- Create outline

During

- Use outline to guide conversation
- Record show
- Mention advertisers, sponsors, etc.
- Promote your product or service
- Call-to-action for listeners

After

- Edit show
- Upload show to RSS feed (hosting site)
- Send thank you email to guest
- Promote show and repurpose content

Note: See back section of this journal for templates, outlines and guides.

For more resources, visit www.MotorCityWoman.com

Month: _____

What are your goals for this month?
_____
_____
_____
_____

How many show are you doing this month? ☐

Show: _____
Topic: _____
Guest: _____

Show: _____
Topic: _____
Guest: _____

Show: _____
Topic: _____
Guest: _____

Show: _____
Topic: _____
Guest: _____

Show: _____
Topic: _____
Guest: _____

For more resources, visit www.MotorCityWoman.com

Intentions Page

Success doesn't happen by accident. Use this space to set your intention or plan of action to achieve a successful podcast.

Punch List for each show

It can sometimes get difficult to do everything for each show. Luckily, you have this planner to keep you organized!

Before

- Identify show topic
- Confirm guest and recording date
- Send guest prep email
- Create outline

During

- Use outline to guide conversation
- Record show
- Mention advertisers, sponsors, etc.
- Promote your product or service
- Call-to-action for listeners

After

- Edit show
- Upload show to RSS feed (hosting site)
- Send thank you email to guest
- Promote show and repurpose content

Note: See back section of this journal for templates, outlines and guides.

For more resources, visit www.MotorCityWoman.com

I've learned that people will forget what you said, people will forget what you did, but people will never forget how you made them feel.

- MAYA ANGELOU

For more resources, visit www.MotorCityWoman.com

Month: ☐

What are your goals for this month?
_____
_____
_____

How many show are you doing this month? ☐

Show: _____
Topic: _____
Guest: _____

Show: _____
Topic: _____
Guest: _____

Show: _____
Topic: _____
Guest: _____

Show: _____
Topic: _____
Guest: _____

Show: _____
Topic: _____
Guest: _____

For more resources, visit www.MotorCityWoman.com

Intentions Page

Success doesn't happen by accident. Use this space to set your intention or plan of action to achieve a successful podcast.

_____
_____
_____
_____
_____
_____
_____
_____
_____
_____
_____
_____
_____
_____
_____
_____
_____
_____
_____
_____
_____
_____
_____
_____
_____

Punch List for each show

It can sometimes get difficult to do everything for each show. Luckily, you have this planner to keep you organized!

Before

- ☐ Identify show topic
- ☐ Confirm guest and recording date
- ☐ Send guest prep email
- ☐ Create outline

During

- ☐ Use outline to guide conversation
- ☐ Record show
- ☐ Mention advertisers, sponsors, etc.
- ☐ Promote your product or service
- ☐ Call-to-action for listeners

After

- ☐ Edit show
- ☐ Upload show to RSS feed (hosting site)
- ☐ Send thank you email to guest
- ☐ Promote show and repurpose content

Note: See back section of this journal for templates, outlines and guides.

> Words mean more than what is set down on paper. It takes the human voice to infuse them with shades of deeper meaning.
>
> - MAYA ANGELOU

For more resources, visit www.MotorCityWoman.com

Month: _____

What are your goals for this month?
_____
_____
_____
_____

How many show are you doing this month? ☐

Show: _____
Topic: _____
Guest: _____

Show: _____
Topic: _____
Guest: _____

Show: _____
Topic: _____
Guest: _____

Show: _____
Topic: _____
Guest: _____

Show: _____
Topic: _____
Guest: _____

For more resources, visit www.MotorCityWoman.com

Intentions Page

Success doesn't happen by accident. Use this space to set your intention or plan of action to achieve a successful podcast.

_____
_____
_____
_____
_____
_____
_____
_____
_____
_____
_____
_____
_____
_____
_____
_____
_____
_____
_____
_____
_____
_____
_____
_____

Punch List for each show

It can sometimes get difficult to do everything for each show. Luckily, you have this planner to keep you organized!

Before

- Identify show topic
- Confirm guest and recording date
- Send guest prep email
- Create outline

During

- Use outline to guide conversation
- Record show
- Mention advertisers, sponsors, etc.
- Promote your product or service
- Call-to-action for listeners

After

- Edit show
- Upload show to RSS feed (hosting site)
- Send thank you email to guest
- Promote show and repurpose content

Note: See back section of this journal for templates, outlines and guides.

For more resources, visit www.MotorCityWoman.com

I am not afraid to use my voice. My thoughts, opinions and ideas are important.

- AUTHOR UNKNOWN

For more resources, visit www.MotorCityWoman.com

Month: ⬜

What are your goals for this month?
_____
_____
_____
_____

How many show are you doing this month? ⬜

Show: _____
Topic: _____
Guest: _____

Show: _____
Topic: _____
Guest: _____

Show: _____
Topic: _____
Guest: _____

Show: _____
Topic: _____
Guest: _____

Show: _____
Topic: _____
Guest: _____

Intentions Page

Success doesn't happen by accident. Use this space to set your intention or plan of action to achieve a successful podcast.

Punch List for each show

It can sometimes get difficult to do everything for each show. Luckily, you have this planner to keep you organized!

Before

- [ ] Identify show topic
- [ ] Confirm guest and recording date
- [ ] Send guest prep email
- [ ] Create outline

During

- [ ] Use outline to guide conversation
- [ ] Record show
- [ ] Mention advertisers, sponsors, etc.
- [ ] Promote your product or service
- [ ] Call-to-action for listeners

After

- [ ] Edit show
- [ ] Upload show to RSS feed (hosting site)
- [ ] Send thank you email to guest
- [ ] Promote show and repurpose content

Note: See back section of this journal for templates, outlines and guides.

For more resources, visit www.MotorCityWoman.com

Month: ☐

What are your goals for this month?
_____
_____
_____
_____

How many show are you doing this month? ☐

Show: _____
Topic: _____
Guest: _____

Show: _____
Topic: _____
Guest: _____

Show: _____
Topic: _____
Guest: _____

Show: _____
Topic: _____
Guest: _____

Show: _____
Topic: _____
Guest: _____

For more resources, visit www.MotorCityWoman.com

Intentions Page

Success doesn't happen by accident. Use this space to set your intention or plan of action to achieve a successful podcast.

Punch List for each show

It can sometimes get difficult to do everything for each show. Luckily, you have this planner to keep you organized!

Before

- Identify show topic
- Confirm guest and recording date
- Send guest prep email
- Create outline

During

- Use outline to guide conversation
- Record show
- Mention advertisers, sponsors, etc.
- Promote your product or service
- Call-to-action for listeners

After

- Edit show
- Upload show to RSS feed (hosting site)
- Send thank you email to guest
- Promote show and repurpose content

Note: See back section of this journal for templates, outlines and guides.

When I dare to be powerful – to use my strength in the service of my vision, then it becomes less and less important whether I am afraid.

- AUDRE LORDE

For more resources, visit www.MotorCityWoman.com

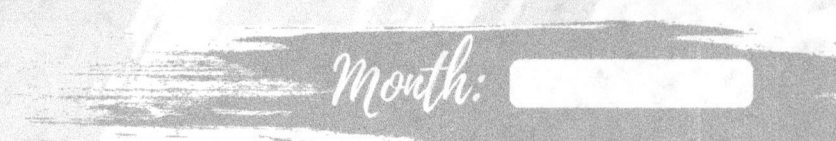

Month: _____

What are your goals for this month?
_____
_____
_____
_____

How many show are you doing this month? ☐

Show: _____
Topic: _____
Guest: _____

Show: _____
Topic: _____
Guest: _____

Show: _____
Topic: _____
Guest: _____

Show: _____
Topic: _____
Guest: _____

Show: _____
Topic: _____
Guest: _____

Intentions Page

Success doesn't happen by accident. Use this space to set your intention or plan of action to achieve a successful podcast.

Punch List for each show

It can sometimes get difficult to do everything for each show. Luckily, you have this planner to keep you organized!

Before

- Identify show topic
- Confirm guest and recording date
- Send guest prep email
- Create outline

During

- Use outline to guide conversation
- Record show
- Mention advertisers, sponsors, etc.
- Promote your product or service
- Call-to-action for listeners

After

- Edit show
- Upload show to RSS feed (hosting site)
- Send thank you email to guest
- Promote show and repurpose content

Note: See back section of this journal for templates, outlines and guides.

For more resources, visit www.MotorCityWoman.com

Month:

What are your goals for this month?
_____
_____
_____
_____

How many show are you doing this month? ☐

Show: _____
Topic: _____
Guest: _____

Show: _____
Topic: _____
Guest: _____

Show: _____
Topic: _____
Guest: _____

Show: _____
Topic: _____
Guest: _____

Show: _____
Topic: _____
Guest: _____

Intentions Page

Success doesn't happen by accident. Use this space to set your intention or plan of action to achieve a successful podcast.

Punch List for each show

It can sometimes get difficult to do everything for each show. Luckily, you have this planner to keep you organized!

Before

- Identify show topic
- Confirm guest and recording date
- Send guest prep email
- Create outline

During

- Use outline to guide conversation
- Record show
- Mention advertisers, sponsors, etc.
- Promote your product or service
- Call-to-action for listeners

After

- Edit show
- Upload show to RSS feed (hosting site)
- Send thank you email to guest
- Promote show and repurpose content

Note: See back section of this journal for templates, outlines and guides.

For more resources, visit www.MotorCityWoman.com

> There's power in allowing yourself to be known and heard, in owning your unique story, in using your authentic voice.
>
> - MICHELLE OBAMA

For more resources, visit www.MotorCityWoman.com

 **Month:**

What are your goals for this month?
_____
_____
_____
_____

How many show are you doing this month? [ ]

Show: _____
Topic: _____
Guest: _____

Show: _____
Topic: _____
Guest: _____

Show: _____
Topic: _____
Guest: _____

Show: _____
Topic: _____
Guest: _____

Show: _____
Topic: _____
Guest: _____

Intentions Page

Success doesn't happen by accident. Use this space to set your intention or plan of action to achieve a successful podcast.

Punch List for each show

It can sometimes get difficult to do everything for each show. Luckily, you have this planner to keep you organized!

Before

- Identify show topic
- Confirm guest and recording date
- Send guest prep email
- Create outline

During

- Use outline to guide conversation
- Record show
- Mention advertisers, sponsors, etc.
- Promote your product or service
- Call-to-action for listeners

After

- Edit show
- Upload show to RSS feed (hosting site)
- Send thank you email to guest
- Promote show and repurpose content

Note: See back section of this journal for templates, outlines and guides.

For more resources, visit www.MotorCityWoman.com

Great shows start with a desire to serve.

- ROBIN KINNIE

For more resources, visit www.MotorCityWoman.com

Month:

What are your goals for this month?
_____
_____
_____
_____

How many show are you doing this month? [ ]

Show: _____
Topic: _____
Guest: _____

Show: _____
Topic: _____
Guest: _____

Show: _____
Topic: _____
Guest: _____

Show: _____
Topic: _____
Guest: _____

Show: _____
Topic: _____
Guest: _____

For more resources, visit www.MotorCityWoman.com

Intentions Page

Success doesn't happen by accident. Use this space to set your intention or plan of action to achieve a successful podcast.

Punch List for each show

It can sometimes get difficult to do everything for each show. Luckily, you have this planner to keep you organized!

Before

- Identify show topic
- Confirm guest and recording date
- Send guest prep email
- Create outline

During

- Use outline to guide conversation
- Record show
- Mention advertisers, sponsors, etc.
- Promote your product or service
- Call-to-action for listeners

After

- Edit show
- Upload show to RSS feed (hosting site)
- Send thank you email to guest
- Promote show and repurpose content

Note: See back section of this journal for templates, outlines and guides.

For more resources, visit www.MotorCityWoman.com

SAMPLE SHOW OUTLINE

TITLE

DATE   **GUEST**

- Beginning
1. Theme for this episode (what are we talking about?)
2. Introduction of Guest, if applicable or Monologue
3. Why is this important?

- Middle
1. Core topic items
2. Main 3 guest questions
3. Promo or ad for event, product or service

- Closing
1. Summarize key take-aways
2. Share contact information
3. Direct call-to-action (what do you want the listener to do? Visit your site, follow you on social media, subscribe to your newsletter) BE CLEAR
4. Signature closing

For more resources, visit www.MotorCityWoman.com

Motor City Woman
PODCAST SOCIAL MEDIA STRATEGY GUIDE

1. PICK YOUR #1 PLATFORM
You don't have to be active on every social media platform. Go where your audience is.

2. IDENTITY
Decide if your podcast will have its' own identity or be part of an existing brand.

3. MIX IT UP!
No one wants to only see posts for new episodes. Highlight your personality and core values.

4. BEHIND THE SCENES
Incorporate pictures and video to show listeners production outtakes, audiograms and guests.

FOR MORE TOOLS VISIT OUR YOUTUBE CHANNEL

For more resources, visit www.MotorCityWoman.com

Finding Great Guests

- Facebook groups
- Ask! Post on social media for topic experts
- Follow hashtags on Twitter and Instagram for thought leaders
- Research trade associations
- Identify experts through your local Chamber of Commerce
- Go through Eventbrite to see who is hosting events related to your topic and scout speakers
- Your personal network
- Cross-promote by inviting a fellow podcaster to be your guest
- Use LinkedIn groups to network
- Search key words on Pinterest
- Help A Reporter Out (HARO)
- Mastermind groups
- Include a referral form in your guest thank you email

For more resources, visit www.MotorCityWoman.com

Sample Prospective Guest Email

Hi,
My name is XXX and I am the Host of XXX show. My show (purpose of show). Here is a link to previous episodes (link). We reach an audience of (stats) with topics ranging from XX to XX. I would like to interview you because (why?). I look forward to hearing from you soon.

If YES:

Thank you for your response. In order to produce the best show, I've put together a few guiding questions. Feel free to complete the questions (link to Google doc) and upload your short bio and headshot (link to Google drive). Finally, you can select which recording dates work best for you here (link to Calendly). (Attach consent form)

Follow-up Email Confirmation

Hi XX,
We are all set to record on (date and time). Click (here) for the address to the studio (or link for remote recording). To get the best audio quality, I recommend the following:

1. Find a quiet spot indoors
2. Use earbuds or headphones with mic attachment
3. Call in via phone if you have a weak WIFI signal
4. Arrive 5-10 minutes early for soundcheck

I'm looking forward to speaking with you soon!

Thank you Email

Hi XX,
Thank you for being a guest on (name of show). Here is a link to the recording. I have attached a graphic that you can use to promote your appearance. My goal (mission of show). If you are interested in supporting the show, I have attached our current advertising and sponsorship packages. Additionally, feel free to recommend others for guest consideration.

How To Repurpose Content

The secret of most marketers is to repurpose content. By repurposing content, you are able to reach potential listeners in different ways. What works on one platform make not work on another.

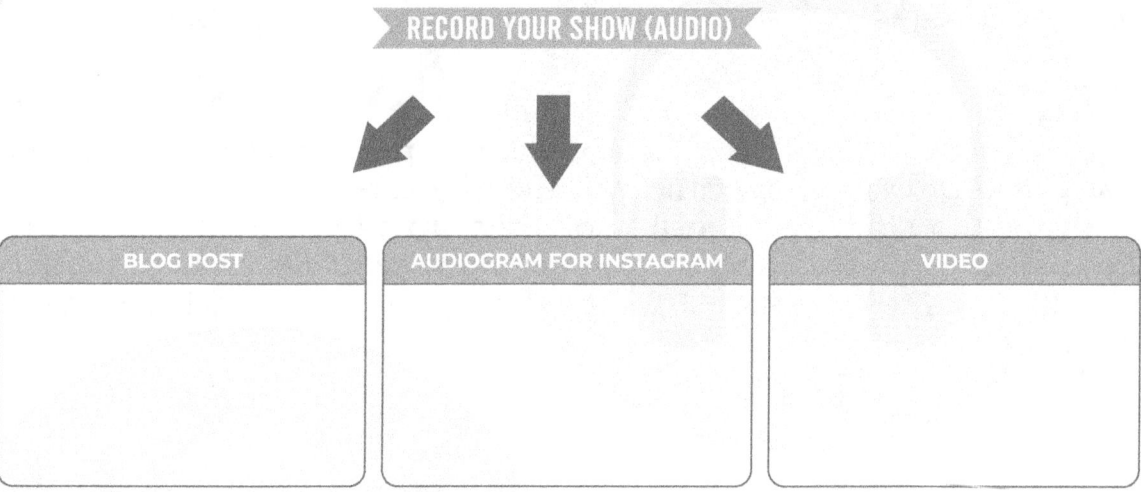

Transcribe your show into a **blog post.** This gives you the opportunity to sell affiliate links and drive traffic to your website. It will also be a recap of the show and call-to-action.

Audiograms can be shared on social media when you may not have a picture of you and your guest. An audiogram using sites like headliner or waave can emphasize a quote from your guest or a funny exchange.

Release a **video** version of your show to grow your YouTube channel. YouTube is proving to be a search engine for people looking for resources so, take advantage! It captures a different audience and aligns with the #1 marketing format: video.

For more resources, visit www.MotorCityWoman.com

Monetization Strategies

Monetization (def.) the action or process of earning revenue from an asset, business, etc.

With a consistent track record and library of shows, you can now begin exploring monetization for your show which means earning money through your show. Here are some ideas to consider:

Merchandise: branded podcasts

- Buttons
- Stickers
- Hats

Affiliate links: link to service providers/ product sites. For every link, you receive a commission

Sponsorship: Long-term financial supporter

Advertisers: Short-term ads

Live events: Great way to partner with local venues/small businesses

Public fundraising ex. GoFundMe : Grow your community and ask them to support your podcast

Subscription / Membership: Provide an exclusive benefit in exchange for financial support

www.ingramcontent.com/pod-product-compliance
Lightning Source LLC
Chambersburg PA
CBHW081156290426
44108CB00018B/2578